20th Century
PERSPECTIVES

Weapons and Technology of
World War I

Paul Dowswell

Heinemann Library
Chicago, Illinois

Produced for Heinemann Library by Discovery Books Limited
Designed by Sabine Beaupré
Illustrations by Mark Franklin
Maps by Stefan Chabluk
Consultant: Stewart Ross
Originated by Dot Gradations
Printed by Wing King Tong in Hong Kong

06 05 04 03 02
10 9 8 7 6 5 4 3 2 1

Library of Congress Cataloging-in-Publication Data
Dowswell, Paul.
  Weapons and technology of World War I / Paul Dowswell.
    p. cm. -- (20th-century perspectives)
Includes bibliographical references (p.) and index.
Summary: Examines the changes in weapons and tactics that impacted the
way war was waged during World War I.
  ISBN 1-58810-662-4 (lib. bdg.)   ISBN 1-58810-922-4 (pbk. bdg.)
  1. World War, 1914-1918--Equipment and supplies

Acknowledgments
The author and publishers are grateful to the following for permission to reproduce copyright
material: pp. 4, 15, 19, 21, 26, 39 Hulton Getty; pp. 5, 7, 8, 9, 10, 11, 12, 13, 14, 16, 17, 18, 20,
22, 23, 24, 27, 29, 31, 32, 34, 36 (bottom), 37, 38, 40, 41, 42, 43 Corbis; pp. 25, 28, 33, 35, 36
(top) Peter Newark's Pictures.

Cover photograph reproduced with permission of Corbis.

Every effort has been made to contact copyright holders of any material reproduced in this book.
Any omissions will be rectified in subsequent printings if notice is given to the publisher.

Some words are shown in bold, **like this.** You can find out what
they mean by looking in the glossary.

Contents

A Century of War

World War I began in 1914 and ended in 1918. Today, hardly any of the soldiers and **civilians** caught up in the conflict are still living. Yet the battles they fought and the horrors they endured still haunt us. On the **Western** and **Eastern Fronts** (the areas of conflict between opposing armies) and at other major battlegrounds, men were killed in previously unheard-of numbers.

Changing technology

One reason for the huge number of deaths was that weapons and other military technology had changed significantly over the previous hundred years. These developments completely altered the face of warfare.

An earlier era of warfare had ended at the Battle of Waterloo in Belgium in 1815. Under the eyes of commanders who were positioned to survey the whole field of battle, 72,000 French soldiers fought a combined army of over 100,000 troops from Britain, Prussia, and other places. The armies faced each other in tightly squared formation, wearing brightly colored uniforms. Their **bayonets** were attached to single-shot guns called **muskets.** Their **artillery** fired muzzle-loaded, or front-loaded, cannon balls. **Cavalry** soldiers were the ultimate threat, waiting a distance from the fighting and ready to charge in the hope that the enemy **front line** would scatter or crumble before them.

The Battle of Waterloo, seen here, marked the end of an earlier era of warfare. During the rest of the nineteenth century, every large conflict created developments in weapons and technology.

New developments

About 35 years later, a series of armed conflicts occurred that pointed warfare in a new direction. In the Crimean War (1853–56), **rifles** were used instead of muskets. Their grooved **barrels** gave greater accuracy and range. In the American Civil War (1861–65), barbed wire was first used at the front. The Franco-Prussian War (1870–71) introduced the first machine guns. The Boer War (1899–1902) saw widespread use of rifles fitted with **magazines** that contained several shots, so the guns did not need to be reloaded each time they were fired. Finally, the Russo-Japanese War (1904–05) saw the first use of field telephones on the battlefront, as well as huge **howitzer** guns and giant armored battleships.

All these technological advances meant weapons were deadlier than ever before. At the same time, the armies of some countries had grown much larger and better organized. Opposing **empires** had become rivals in a struggle for power in Europe and beyond (see page 6). Many European nations of the early twentieth century were increasingly hostile toward and suspicious of each other. They were also confident that if war did come, their new weapons would win them victory.

In World War I, cavalry soldiers quickly fell victim to enemy machine guns and artillery. This cavalry unit was made up of men from India, which was then a part of the British Empire.

Send in the cavalry

For thousands of years, cavalry was just as important to armies as were ordinary foot soldiers, or **infantry,** because the armed horsemen were fast and **maneuverable.** But in the face of World War I's ferocious defensive weapons, cavalry charges were disastrous. Some cavalry charges were made in western Europe at the start of the war, but with bad results. In one German charge against British troops, only twelve of the 70 horsemen involved survived.

Cavalry still had a part to play in other areas of the war, however, such as on the more open Eastern Front, and in the Middle East. In Palestine, for example, the New Zealand Mounted Rifles and Australian Light Horse soldiers were used very effectively against their Turkish enemies.

World War I Begins

Rivalry among nations

When World War I began in 1914, Europe was already a continent divided by bitter rivalries over territory and military power. There were two main camps, each committed to defending other allied nations. On one side were Germany, Austria-Hungary, and the Ottoman **Empire,** in an alliance known as the Central Powers. On the other side were France, Russia, and Britain, in a combined force known as the Allies, which the United States would later join.

In June 1914, Archduke Franz Ferdinand of Austria-Hungary and his wife were killed by a Serbian assassin in Bosnia. (This area was ruled by Austria-Hungary, but Serbia wished to control it.) Austria-Hungary declared war on Serbia, and Russia joined the war in Serbia's defense. The conflict then spread to most of the rest of Europe, as other nations were pulled into the war.

When the war began, Japan joined the Allies and attacked German **colonies** in the Far East. In 1915, Italy joined the Allies, and Bulgaria joined the Central Powers. Fighting also spread to German colonies in

This map shows how the nations and empires of Europe, North Africa, and the Middle East allied themselves during World War I. Several battlefronts developed during the course of the conflict: the **Western Front,** *the* **Eastern Front,** *the Balkan Front, and the Middle Eastern Front.*

Africa, New Guinea, and Samoa. The United States joined the Allies in 1917, in response to German attacks on U.S. ships. By then, the war was being fought by nations from all over the world, although most of the fighting took place in Europe, both on land and at sea, and in the Middle East.

Trench tactics

Much of the warfare, at least on the Western Front, took place in trenches, protective ditches from which armies launched attacks on each other. Trenches had first been used this way in the American Civil War. The military planners of World War I chose trench warfare based on their knowledge of earlier conflicts, such as the Battle of Mukden in the Russo-Japanese War. The **casualties** of this four-week battle had been immense: 70,000 Japanese died and 100,000 Russians died. But despite their losses, the Japanese had eventually overwhelmed the Russian trenches. It seemed that all-out attack, whatever the casualties, would eventually win the day.

The World War I generals in Europe envisioned attacks by "waves" of men moving close together in support of each other. Military thinking ruled out taking cover as troops neared enemy positions. It was thought that a steady advance in the face of enemy fire actually produced fewer casualties. Only toward the end of the war did such **tactics** change.

*Allied troops on the Western Front in 1918, led by their commander, leave a trench as German **shells** explode around them. The military tactic of advancing steadily into the face of heavy fire cost countless lives.*

Terrible lessons

In the early weeks of World War I, such actions cost huge numbers of men their lives. It quickly became clear that the weapons of defense, especially the machine gun that could fire a murderous 600 **rounds** a minute, were too powerful for such simple tactics.

As the **front lines** solidified into well-defended trenches, senior commanders on all sides found they were fighting a type of war at which they had no experience and no clear idea of how to win. Their training and experience told them that in warfare, victory lay with the army that could seize ground from the enemy. But if no one could seize ground from anyone else, how could the war be won? The generals spent the next four years trying to solve this problem. Tragically, some of their **strategies** and tactics were more suitable to the previous century than to the changing face of warfare, and resulted in dreadful slaughter.

Trench Warfare

The Western Front

As attacks and **counterattacks** ground to a halt in the autumn of 1914, French and British troops raced to the North Sea and Swiss border in an attempt to **outflank** the Germans, who were doing the same thing in the hope of outflanking the Allies. Both sides failed, but the lands they occupied formed the **Western Front,** which stretched more than 450 miles (720 kilometers) through Belgium and along France's eastern border with Germany.

The Western Front soon developed into a complex series of opposing trenches. These **fortified** ditches had firing steps, sandbag protection, **parapets, dugouts,** their own crude sanitary systems, and even rail supply networks. Sometimes the gap between opposing trenches, known as "no-man's-land," was a half-mile or more wide; sometimes it was as narrow as 100 feet (30 meters). These types of fortifications were also used at other fronts.

Between late 1914 and the spring of 1918, millions of lives were lost on the Western Front trying to break through enemy trenches. But in all that time, the front line never moved more than ten miles (sixteen kilometers) one way or the other. The trenches, defended with machine guns and barbed wire, were virtually impenetrable.

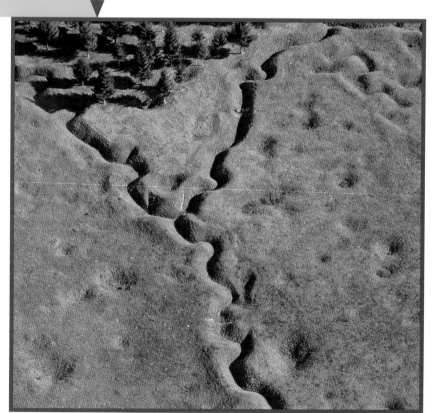

Trench networks

Trenches were usually built in three or more connected lines, with a **front line** trench and two or more support trenches behind it. Behind these were **artillery** positions. Communication trenches connected them so soldiers could move between trenches with a lower risk of being shot.

Ahead of the front line trench were dense rows of barbed wire, often laid in thick, tubular tiers. As defense techniques grew more advanced, the lines of barbed wire would be arranged with deliberate gaps or weak spots. Enemy infantrymen would move to these areas and could be herded into a "killing ground," where machine gun fire would be at its most concentrated.

New techniques

Later in the war, German trenches, and then Allied ones, were arranged with greater sophistication. Instead of a continuous front line trench, there would be a series of small outposts intended to slow down attacking infantry. Behind these was a battle zone full of **strong points.** Even farther back was a line of artillery and machine gun nests. Such deep defenses were even more difficult to attack than the earlier arrangements of trenches.

Barbed wire, invented in 1873, was originally used to replace wooden fencing around grazing land for cattle in the western United States. Used here to protect French troops in their trench, barbed wire proved to be a deadly hindrance to attacking troops.

Forts

Not all of the Western Front was defended by trenches. In some places, especially at the French strong point of Verdun and along the German Hindenburg Line, there were huge, concrete forts. Such fortifications were built to withstand heavy bombardment.

Verdun became the scene of some of the worst fighting of the war. Over a ten-month campaign from February to December 1916, German troops overran Fort Douaumont there, and forced the defenders of Fort Vaux to surrender for lack of water. But the French were grimly determined to hold on to their fortresses. In the end, the Verdun campaign ground to a halt with losses of around a third of a million men on both sides.

Life in the Trenches

The experience of being in the **front line** trenches was so exhausting and terrifying that soldiers were rarely stationed there for more than a week. In any given month, a soldier might also have spent a week in a support trench and two weeks at the rear.

Keeping busy

In the lulls between big battles, there was still constant activity in the trenches. By day, any soldier who showed himself above the trench **parapet** risked instant death, so **periscopes** were often used to keep a watch on enemy activity. These crude wooden boxes were about two feet long, with a reflecting mirror at each end. Their use allowed soldiers to look out while staying hidden, so they saved many lives.

Darkness offered greater protection. At night, men set out into no-man's-land or to the **shell**-pocked craters around their own trenches. There, they repaired gaps in barbed wire or fixed field telephone lines. Sometimes small groups would venture toward enemy lines to check the strength of them or to carry out hit-and-run raids.

We are fairly plagued by rats. They have eaten nearly everything in the mess, including the tablecloth and the operations orders! We borrowed a large cat and shut it up at night to exterminate them, and found the place empty next morning. The rats must have eaten it up, bones, fur, and all, and dragged it to their holes.

P. H. Pilditch, British officer at Ypres, France

Home comforts and trench horrors

Men in the trenches were generally well fed, and were often able to bring some home comforts with them. There was even a postal service so regular and efficient that cakes and other perishable foods could be sent to soldiers from home.

However, most trenches were still miserable places. They needed considerable upkeep, and even this was often not enough to keep them from flooding in the soggy landscape and dreary climate of northern Europe. In winter, rain turned everything to mud. Trenches would sometimes flood to waist level, and soldiers often suffered from a form of frostbite called trench foot. In summer, the heat and flies made the stench of **latrines** and dead bodies unbearable. Huge rats fed on the corpses of men and horses, and soldiers tried to get rid of them by shooting or beating them to death.

[It was] . . . an underground dwelling approached by forty steps hewn into the solid chalk, so that even the heaviest shells at this depth made no more than a pleasant rumble . . . . In one wall I had a bed hewn out . . . . At its head hung an electric light so I could read. The whole was shut off from the outer world by a dark-red curtain with rod and rings.

German soldier Ernst Junger, describing the living quarters in his trench on the Western Front

In their well-built trench on the Western Front in 1915, German soldiers search their clothes for signs of lice. Most men had their hair cut as short as possible to make delousing easier.

Illness and **infestation** spread like wildfire in the trenches. Everyone became plagued by lice within a day or two of front line duty. Not only did the lice cause maddening itching, but they transmitted a debilitating sickness known as trench fever.

In general, French and British trenches were particularly squalid. This was partly due to the Allied leaders' belief that the trenches were temporary, and the war would once again become one of movement. German trenches were much better built and maintained, on the whole. German commanders recognized the permanency of the trenches far sooner, and their men lived in much greater safety and comfort.

Uniforms, Rifles, and Bayonets

Protective clothing

For several hundred years before World War I, many armies had worn bright, colorful uniforms. Such outfits clearly identified the wearers, especially in the terror and confusion of hand-to-hand fighting. Uniforms also enabled commanders overlooking a battle to have a clear idea of where their troops were. But by the early twentieth century, such conspicuous outfits were used much less often. Most armies were issued uniforms of duller fabrics, to better conceal them from their enemies.

Even in 1914, French soldiers still wore blue tunics and bright red trousers, and regarded their German enemy's drab gray uniforms with disdain. The British army wore khaki, although Scottish regiments were allowed to wear tartan kilts. As the war dragged on, however, the French discarded their bright uniforms, and even the Scots took to covering their kilts with a khaki outer skirt. The truth had become obvious: the less a man could be seen, the less likely he was to be shot.

The soldiers who fought in World War I were as varied as their uniforms, but most carried rifles. This group of irregular soldiers from Bulgaria fought on the Balkan Front. Bulgaria was allied to the Central Powers and invaded Serbia in 1915.

Soft peaked caps were also replaced with heavy metal helmets during the course of the war. Despite their obvious use in protecting soldiers' heads from **shell** and **shrapnel** fragments, helmets were not popular with everyone because they were uncomfortable to wear.

Infantry weapons

The main weapon for all **infantry** in the war was the **rifle.** The Germans, for example, had the Mauser Gewehr 98; the British had the 1907 Lee-Enfield; and the Americans had the M1903 Springfield. All of these weapons were of similar type and quality. They all had a bolt action, meaning that the user pulled back a bolt in the rifle to empty one **round** from the firing chamber and load a fresh one. They all had **magazines** that allowed the user to fire off several shots rapidly without the need to reload. They were all accurate to at least 600 yards (550 meters), but some could fire around 3,000 yards (2,700 meters).

"The spirit of the bayonet"

When an infantryman went into battle, he attached a **bayonet** to the end of his rifle, effectively turning it into a spear. Different armies had their own distinctive bayonets. The British type was like a knife blade, the French style more like a thin needle (which broke easily), and the Germans used a blade with a serrated edge.

Instructors talked about "the spirit of the bayonet," meaning the courage and determination a soldier should show in killing his enemy by the terribly intimate method of stabbing him. Soldiers were told that their enemies had a particular fear of the bayonet (as if any man wouldn't), and that its enthusiastic use gave them a **psychological** advantage over their foe.

A French corporal suddenly stood before me, both our bayonets at the ready, he to kill me, I to kill him. Pushing his weapon aside I stabbed him in the chest. He dropped his rifle and fell . . . . I stood over him for a few seconds and then I gave him the coup de grâce ["finishing stroke"]. After we had taken the enemy position, I felt giddy, my knees shook, and I was actually sick.

German army corporal Stephan Westman, describing hand-to-hand fighting

These U.S. soldiers fire rifles at the enemy from their trench in France in 1918. Their rifles were equipped with bayonets for use in fighting hand-to-hand, especially when there was a risk of hitting their own side with rifle fire.

Other Weapons of Trench Warfare

*This World War I poster shows a U.S. soldier about to throw a grenade into a German trench. Posters such as these were used to encourage **civilians** to support the war effort by buying **war bonds.***

Grenades

Grenades had been used effectively in the Russo-Japanese War, and were enthusiastically taken up by the German army in World War I. They were little metal cases packed with explosives, light enough to be thrown by a man. There were two basic types. German troops mostly used a type that looked like a metal **canister** on a stick, such as the *Stielhandgranate*. The British and French used smaller round or oval-shaped grenades, such as the Mills bomb.

Some grenades were designed to explode on impact, but most had a timed **fuse** of around five seconds. Using them required great skill and courage. Thrown too soon, they could be caught and thrown back before exploding. Also, the act of throwing often exposed a soldier to enemy fire, since he had to come out of the trench to toss accurately.

Lend *the way they* **Fight**

Buy Bonds *to your* **UTMOST**

The British and French armies were much slower than the Germans in introducing grenades. To compensate for this, Allied troops took to making their own by packing explosives, nails, and scrap metal into empty tin cans. Grenades were tremendously effective, and eventually became the favored weapon of infantrymen in trench warfare.

Field mortars

Once the war had settled into a **stalemate,** another new weapon was introduced: the tubelike field mortar. A kind of portable, miniature **howitzer,** a mortar such as the British Stokes was light enough to be carried by a small team of men. One French mortar, the Crapouillot, could even be carried on one man's back.

Mortars were extremely useful. Firing almost straight into the air, in a nearly vertical **trajectory,** they could deliver high explosives, **shrapnel,** smoke bombs, and even poison gas **shells** from one trench to another.

Flamethrowers

One of the most terrible trench weapons, the flamethrower, used pressurized gas from a canister to project a mixture of burning oil and gasoline. Although devices that projected fire had been used since ancient times, the flamethrower as we know it today was invented in Germany in 1906. The idea was also adopted by both the British and French armies.

Heavy flamethrowers, such as the British Livens, were installed in some trenches, but were impractical. They used vast amounts of precious fuel and were too cumbersome to be moved effectively. Much more useful were portable flamethrowers with smaller gas canisters, such as the German Kleif and Wex, and the French Schilt. These were light enough to be carried by one man, and could be employed in enemy trenches, where they were murderously effective.

Mines

One type of warfare on the **Western Front** involved the digging of mines, or underground tunnels, to enemy trenches. Army construction workers, many of whom had previously been coal miners or had dug tunnels for underground rail networks in Europe's capitals, were sent to dig underneath the enemy **front lines.** Huge amounts of explosives were then planted at the ends of the tunnels. There were many dangers involved in this work, and the fear of being buried alive in a collapsing tunnel was always present. Also, the enemy would sometimes burrow into these tunnels, and miners faced the terrifying prospect of fighting underground gun battles.

It took the Allies two years to dig the tunnels that reached under the German trenches at Messines in France. There, about 500 tons of explosives were **detonated** on June 7, 1917. Shock-waves from the explosion could be felt in central London, several hundred miles away.

A German assault force attacks using flamethrowers. The job of a flamethrower operator required a special kind of courage. He would be a priority target for enemy troops, and his own highly flammable load could easily explode, enveloping him with burning fuel.

Machine Guns

Aside from the squalor of the trenches, no other image seems to symbolize World War I so starkly as that of the machine gun. Perched atop a trench **parapet** and operated by two or more men, it could shoot a lethal ribbon of bullets at attacking troops. **Artillery** killed more soldiers overall, but those deaths were caused by **shells** fired from far behind the lines. The contact between a machine gunner and his victims was much more immediate and personal.

An efficient killing machine

With an average rate of fire of around 600 **rounds** a minute, the machine gun could kill more efficiently than any other weapon of the time. On the first day of the Battle of the Somme on the **Western Front** in 1916, German machine guns cut down 60,000 British soldiers. Machine guns also proved invaluable in battles on other fronts. In 1914, at Tannenburg (in what is now Poland) on the **Eastern Front,** German gunners massacred the advancing Russian army. At Gallipoli (in present-day Turkey), units from Australia and New Zealand were devastated by Turkish gunners in 1915.

A French machine gun crew is poised for action with their Hotchkiss machine gun in 1915. The Hotchkiss was one of the principal machine guns used in World War I.

Machine gun crews

The main machine guns used in the war—the German Maxim MG '08, the British Vickers Mk 1, the French Hotchkiss, the Russian Sokolov, and the American Browning—were fairly standard in their performance. Their individual effectiveness depended very much on the skill of the crews that operated them.

Many guns used a team of several men to operate them. In one common six-man group, one would fire as a second would carefully feed in the bullets that were held in a metal or fabric strip. Two other men would keep them supplied with **ammunition.** This pair also kept the barrel of the gun cool in a water jacket so that it wouldn't overheat and stop working. Another two men would act as scouts. They doubled as personal guards for the gunner, who could expect no mercy if he fell into the hands of attacking troops.

Prewar development

The machine gun was developed during the late 1800s by American Hiram Maxim. It first earned its fearsome reputation in small-scale **colonial** wars between European powers and African and Asian countries. By the time World War I broke out, French military planners estimated that one machine gun was as effective as 150 or even 200 **rifles.**

Lighter weapons

At the start of World War I, most machine guns were too heavy to be carried around, so their use was restricted to trench defense. But their effectiveness encouraged the development of more portable machine guns, such as the German Madsen and British Lewis gun.

By the end of the war, the Germans had developed the first submachine gun, the Bergmann MP 18. This gun could be carried by a single infantryman, and could fire 540 rounds a minute, almost as many as a heavy machine gun. The gunner had to be careful how he used it, however. The drum that carried its bullets only held 32 rounds, and these could be fired off in less than four seconds.

By the time U.S. soldiers entered World War I in 1917, smaller machine guns were being developed. These were light enough for their crews to carry them into battle alongside attacking infantrymen.

The Power of Artillery

A major offensive weapon

Soldiers had good reason to fear **artillery.** These large guns fired **shells,** or metal cases of various shapes containing explosives or other lethal materials. Over 70 percent of all **casualties** in World War I were caused by shell fire. One German statistic estimated that artillery killed fourteen of the enemy for every one killed by **infantry.** Yet this killing power was bought at a massive material cost: other statistics from the war suggest that more than 1,000 shells were used for every actual death by artillery.

Until the arrival of the tank, artillery was the major **offensive** weapon of World War I. It was artillery shells that created the treeless and cratered landscape of no man's land. Because of its effectiveness and importance, artillery took up a huge part of most armies' resources and effort. By the end of the war, the British army, for example, had half a million soldiers in its artillery units. On the **home front,** 70 percent of all British factory workers were employed in the **munitions** industry.

New developments

Most armies' artillery units used highly efficient weapons, although the Russian army occasionally used guns that dated back to the Crimean War of 1853–56. By the time of World War I, guns were mostly breech-loaded, meaning that shells were placed in the back and fired out of the front—a much more efficient system than that of the old muzzle-loaded artillery.

These guns also had **barrel**-only recoil. A mechanism inside the gun allowed only the barrel to move back, or recoil, when the shell fired. The rest of the

*Artillery bombardments were lethally effective. Here, British soldiers fire 20-cm **howitzers** during the Battle of the Somme in 1916. In this battle, well over a million soldiers were killed in four months, with this high death rate due in large part to new and more powerful artillery.*

gun stayed in exactly the same position. Guns like these did not need to be re-aimed after every firing.

Deadly shells

The effect of these developments was that a trained crew could fire as many as fifteen or more heavy shells a minute. The shells used in World War I were filled mostly with one of three materials. High explosives would usually **detonate** on impact. **Shrapnel** shells had timed **fuses** that would usually cause the shells to detonate in midair, raining down lethal metal balls on enemy soldiers below. And by the end of the war, more than a quarter of all shells fired by artillery contained poisonous gas rather than explosives.

These French troops duck under shell fire at the Battle of Verdun in 1916. Millions of shells were fired during the ten-month battle.

Artillery weapons

There were several types of artillery weapons. These are the main ones:

Artillery guns fired low **trajectory,** high **velocity** shells over a long range. They were usually of two types: the field gun and the heavy gun. Field guns, such as the French 1897 75 mm and British Mk 1 18-pounder, were the lighter type, and were used nearer the **front line.** Heavy guns, such as the German 17 cm and French 220 mm Schneider, were difficult to move but were more effective, especially against deep **bunkers** and concrete **fortifications.**

Howitzers, including guns such as the French 520 mm Schneider and the German "Big Bertha" 42 cm, fired heavy shells on a high, short-range trajectory. The shells arrived with a terrifying whistle, but at least that gave warning of their approach.

Siege guns, huge weapons usually mounted on rails, could fire a 200-pound (90-kilogram) shell more than 70 miles (110 kilometers). A few of these were used to attack the French capital of Paris from behind German lines. Accuracy declined rapidly after the first twenty shells, so the barrels had to be replaced regularly.

Using the New Artillery

World War I generals were forced to place their highly skilled and valuable **artillery** crews out of range of enemy **rifle** fire. However, it was difficult to fire artillery with full effectiveness away from the **front line.** Artillery commanders had to rely on spotters who could observe where the **shells** were landing and then relay the information by field telephone or even **semaphore.** Later in the war, aerial spotters would radio this information from above the action. Generally, the solution was simply to fire more shells to compensate for the lack of accuracy caused by distance.

An Allied 36-cm artillery gun fires off a shell with a huge blast in Argonne, France. The shell could travel 30 miles (48 kilometers) to German positions, but it was hard to know exactly where it would land.

The military planners had great hopes for their sophisticated artillery weapons. They hoped these would break through the enemy barbed wire that was so effective in keeping soldiers from advancing. But barbed wire was surprisingly resistant to shell blasts. Shots that landed in the wire-strewn "killing zone" ahead of the front line blasted craters into the ground, but the wire simply fell back into these, unbroken.

Creeping barrages

It was also hoped that artillery would be able to protect soldiers as they advanced toward enemy trenches. A "creeping **barrage**" could be laid down, where shells would fall in front of the troops as they slowly moved forward across no man's land. But in the days before effective radio communication, it was impossible to delay a barrage if troops became bogged down or were caught in enemy fire before they reached the best position behind the curtain of shell fire.

Gun positions

Artillery units did their best to camouflage their positions, and guns were placed so that if one was hit, exploding **ammunition** would not destroy other guns around it. However, concealment became much more difficult after the arrival of **reconnaissance** planes. The Germans became skilled at dropping gas shells onto French and British artillery positions.

Making munitions

On the **home fronts** of the fighting nations, the need for vast numbers of shells put great demands on both production and transportation systems. A British navy **blockade** cut off German supplies of nitrates, essential ingredients for high explosives. But German chemist Fritz Haber developed a process to extract nitrates from atmospheric nitrogen (quite literally out of the air), and Germany was able to continue with shell production.

To make up the numbers of workers needed, women were encouraged to take positions in **munitions** factories. Many thousands joined the work force in manufacturing jobs that had previously been reserved for men. Earning money and enjoying the freedom that an independent income provided was a new experience for many women.

Women in World War I factories proved themselves to be productive and efficient workers—much to the surprise of men, who thought women were incapable of such industrial tasks.

Dear Wilhelm,
I send you greetings from my grave in the earth. We shall soon become mad with this awful artillery fire. Day and night it goes on without ceasing. We sit all day deep down in the earth, with neither light nor sunshine, just waiting for death, which may reach us any moment.

Letter home from a German soldier of the Third Magdeburg Regiment, in a trench on the **Western Front,** autumn 1916

Even if the gas did not directly harm the gun crews, it was much more difficult for them to load and fire their guns when they were wearing gas masks.

Yet for all its fearsome killing power, artillery was never truly able to do what it was supposed to do: bombard enemy trenches and barbed wire into such a pulp that advancing troops would meet no resistance. Trenches, especially German ones, were just too well built to be destroyed by simple explosives.

Poisonous Gas

This view from an airplane shows a lethal cloud of gas heading toward the enemy as Germans launch a gas attack on the Eastern Front.

A new weapon

Poisonous gas was one of the few completely new types of weapons used in World War I. It rarely killed its victims: a mere three percent of gas **casualties** actually died on the battlefield. But it was so effective at disabling troops that by 1918, about 25 percent of British **shells** and 80 percent of German shells carried gas instead of high explosives.

The Germans, at the time world leaders in chemical science, were the first to use gas as a weapon. In January 1915, they released poison gas from **canisters** at Bolimov on the **Eastern Front.** Strong winds and wet weather made this first use ineffective, but when gas was unleashed in more favorable conditions on the **Western Front,** it caused panic in Allied trenches. France and Britain **retaliated** with their own gas attacks shortly afterward.

Types of gases

The first gas used was chlorine. It caused choking and vomiting, and could be fatal if inhaled in sufficient quantity. Phosgene followed within the year, and produced similar symptoms. Like chlorine, it could be released from canisters placed on the **front line,** but it could also be carried in shells.

Deadliest of all was dichlorethylsulphide, known as mustard gas, introduced in 1917. Carried mainly by shells, it would linger where it fell for days. Anyone who came into contact with it would suffer blistered and burned skin and lungs, and often blindness, followed by a slow, choking death by **pneumonia.** Other gases were effective only when inhaled, but mustard gas attacked the skin and would penetrate through uniforms to do its horrible work. Its low battlefield kill rate disguised the fact that many gas victims ended up crippled for life, or died lingering deaths in the years following the war.

No real advantage

Gas had disadvantages as a weapon. A strong wind could blow it back to the very men who had released it, and in wet weather it would gather uselessly near ground level. Fighting for both attackers and defenders was much more difficult in the protective clothing both sides were forced to wear. Gas gave neither side in the war an advantage; it just made life at the front line more horrible for everyone concerned.

As the use of poison gas became more widespread, protective measures improved. At first, troops used goggles and mouth pads soaked in chemicals. Later, hoods and face masks with air filters were developed, for both people and horses.

Gas attack

British war poet Wilfred Owen captured the horror of a gas attack in one of his most famous poems, *Dulce et Decorum Est,* meaning "it is sweet and honorable." (The rest of this Latin phrase is *pro patria mori,* meaning "to die for one's country.") The poem depicts exhausted troops trudging away from the front line *drunk with fatigue; deaf even to the hoots of gas-shells dropping softly behind.*

Owen then describes the terror of the actual attack:

Gas! Gas! Quick, boys!—An ecstasy of fumbling,
Fitting the clumsy helmets just in time,
But someone still was yelling out and stumbling . . .
Dim through the misty panes and thick green light,
As under a green sea, I saw him drowning.

In all my dreams, before my helpless sight,
He plunges at me, guttering, choking, drowning.

Finally, he tells of the awful after-effects the gas has on its luckless victim:

. . . watch the white eyes writhing in his face,
His hanging face, like a devil's sick of sin;
If you could hear, at every jolt, the blood
Come gargling from his froth-corrupted lungs,
Obscene as cancer, bitter as the cud
Of vile, incurable sores on innocent tongues . . .

Transportation

The first automobile took to the road in 1886, nearly 30 years before the outbreak of World War I. But modern armies were slow to make use of motorized transportation, and most continued to make heavy use of horse-drawn vehicles throughout the war.

Railroad travel

The armies of World War I also relied on trains, both to move soldiers close to the fighting and to keep them supplied at the front. In Germany, the rail system had been constructed with a view to moving troops speedily to the nation's borders.

On the **Western Front,** and on the German side of the **Eastern Front,** rail lines functioned efficiently throughout the war. Standard gauge steam engines—those that ran on tracks 56.5 inches (143.5 centimeters) wide—would pull their cars to railheads behind the **front lines.** There, troops and supplies would be dropped off to make their way to the front by other vehicles or on foot. There were also light railways constructed to take supplies from the railhead to just behind the front. These had a smaller gauge track that was much easier and cheaper to build than the ordinary standard gauge.

Motor vehicles

Motorized vehicles designed for other purposes were also used at the front. Parisian taxis ferried thousands of French soldiers out to fight the Germans in the first frantic weeks of the war. By the time the war ended, many trucks, staff cars, and ambulances had joined horse-drawn vehicles at the front.

Before the days of widespread motorized transportation, the military relied on dogs as well as horses to move equipment. This team of dogs is on its way to the front with the Belgian army, pulling a machine gun.

Essential supplies

As the war lengthened from months to years, good transportation was essential for a constant supply of **munitions,** food, and **reinforcements.** When French soldiers were fighting desperately to hold on to Verdun, one small country road saw supply-packed motor vehicles pass by every fourteen seconds on their way to the front line. The road was dubbed the *Voie Sacrée* (Sacred Way).

In Russia, the most technologically backward of all the major fighting nations, it was another story. Russian troops suffered terribly because their transportation system was so poor. A hurried program of factory building had enabled them to produce arms and **ammunition** on a level close to that of Germany, France, and Britain. But the Russians were unable to transport these weapons to keep their armies supplied. This meant that Russian soldiers often went into battle unarmed, with orders to pick up a **rifle** and ammunition from a fallen comrade during the battle. Such poor planning and organization contributed greatly to the number of revolts among Russian soldiers.

Marching off to war

For many soldiers, the surest way to travel was to march. All generals had calculating tables to tell them how quickly a set number of troops could march from one area to another. They usually assumed a speed of 2.5 to 3 miles (4 to 5 kilometers) per hour, including breaks for resting.

Troops had moved in this way since Roman times, but now there were modern hazards to contend with. Closely packed troops were vulnerable to both **shell** fire and aerial attacks. **Reconnaissance** planes could spot long columns of marching men all too easily. Where possible, troops marched close to walls, trees, or buildings, so the shadows they cast could not be seen from the air.

*Buses were sometimes commandeered from Paris or London to carry shells and supplies. They would be seen trundling down muddy roads close to the front lines. This double-decker bus from London was converted for army use with the addition of **artillery** and wooden siding.*

Tanks

This illustration by Stanley L. Wood shows a British tank, the Mark I, used in warfare for the first time at the Battle of the Somme. The German soldiers stood little chance of defending themselves with only their rifles and grenades.

The tank was the most important **innovation** of World War I. The first tanks of the war look clumsy and somewhat comical compared to the sleek, high-tech war machines we know today. But a picture of a tank can never convey the terror that these lumbering monsters inspired, grinding over no man's land, spitting fire from their armored sides, and causing **front line** troops to flee in fear of being crushed under their clanking tracks. They could thunder across trenches and crush barbed wire, all the while spraying enemy soldiers with machine gun fire or high explosive **shells.**

The first tank

The name "tank" came about during the weapon's development, as its inventors wanted to make the enemy think these vehicles were mobile water tanks. Though initially described by the British as "machine gun destroyers," the word tank stuck.

Lord Kitchener, one of Britain's leading generals in the early part of the war, dismissed tanks as "pretty mechanical toys." Fortunately, other British commanders disagreed, and the new weapon went into production. The first fighting tank was the Mark I, developed in 1915 by a British team under Lt. Col. Ernest Swinton. Its **caterpillar tracks** were much better at crossing difficult terrain than wheels were. France also produced a successful tank, the Renault FT17, soon after the British.

Use in battle

Tanks were first used in battle at the Somme in France on September 15, 1916, when a squadron of 49 tanks was deployed. Eighteen reached the enemy trenches and were immensely effective. But the fact that 31 tanks had broken down or gotten stuck in the mud on the way completely overshadowed any success.

A year later, tanks had another chance to prove their worth. In November 1917, at Cambrai, France, 378 Allied tanks advanced on a 7.5-mile (12-kilometer) front. It was there that the tank earned its reputation as an valuable **offensive** weapon. Earlier that year, about 400,000 men had been killed in a terrible three-month massacre at Passchendaele in Belgium. It was a high price to pay for advancing a small section of the Allied front line by only 5.5 miles (9 kilometers). At Cambrai, the 378 tanks and their attendant **infantry** advanced the same distance in a single day.

Americans were quick to seize on the tank's potential. During World War I, they used British and French tanks in their own armored divisions. The Germans used captured Allied tanks when they could, but had produced only twenty of their own huge A7V tanks before the end of the war. Other principal fighting nations, such as Russia and Italy, had just started making tanks when the war came to an end.

World War I tanks, like this British Mark IV, were slow, going no more than 5 miles (7 kilometers) per hour, but they could climb a steep slope and cross 8-foot (2.5-meter) trenches with their caterpillar tracks.

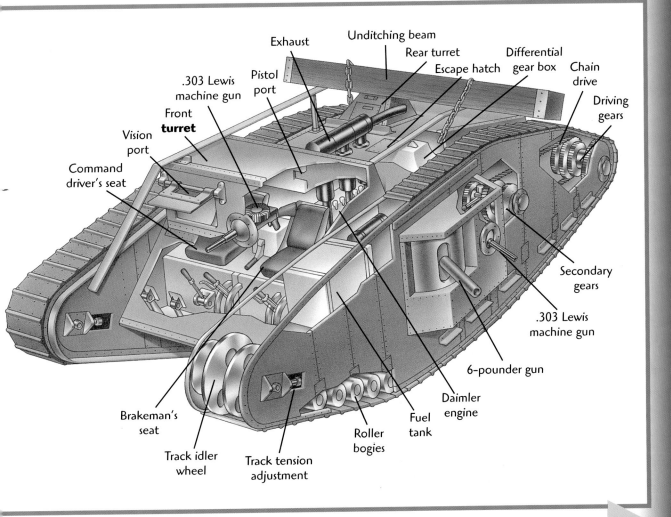

Exhaust
Unditching beam
Rear turret
Escape hatch
Differential gear box
Chain drive
.303 Lewis machine gun
Pistol port
Driving gears
Front **turret**
Vision port
Command driver's seat
Secondary gears
.303 Lewis machine gun
6-pounder gun
Daimler engine
Brakeman's seat
Fuel tank
Roller bogies
Track idler wheel
Track tension adjustment

Mighty Warships

Supremacy at sea

The navies of Britain and Germany had engaged in an expensive arms race before World War I. They built huge battleships called dreadnoughts in a bid to outdo each other as naval powers. At the outbreak of the war, Britain was ahead, with 21 dreadnoughts to Germany's 13.

The British navy had been the most powerful in the world for more than a century. In this period, there had been great technological changes. Warships were now made of steel rather than wood, and were driven by powerful steam **turbine engines.** Their **rifled** guns were held in movable **turrets.** The explosive-packed **shells** they fired could be hurled over distances as great as ten miles (sixteen kilometers). Thanks to intricate range-finding machinery, these shells often found their targets with deadly accuracy.

Warships included several different types. Among them were cruisers (fast, medium-sized ships) and destroyers (small warships used to protect larger ships from attack). Destroyers were well-armed with huge guns and torpedoes. Battleships were the largest and most heavily armed warships, usually clad in heavy **armor plating.** Dreadnoughts were the pride of any fleet. Named after the first of their kind, the British H.M.S. *Dreadnought,* these giant battleships were a devastatingly effective combination of speed and firepower.

The Battle of Jutland

Britain and Germany were both very reluctant to risk their fleets in an all-out battle. The two navies met only once, at the Battle of Jutland in May 1916. During the battle, 6,100 British and 2,550 Germans were killed. Britain lost more ships (fourteen to Germany's ten), but its navy remained very powerful.

Blockade tactics

When the war broke out, both sides used their navies to impose **blockades** on their enemies, to prevent them from importing goods from overseas. In previous wars, blockades had been close to enemy coastlines, but now that accurate torpedoes and explosive-packed mines were major threats, such closeness was impossible. Instead, distant blockades were established.

Britain and France blocked German trade via the North Sea and the Mediterranean. The blockade proved effective. German citizens referred to the winter of 1916–17 as "turnip winter" because food shortages were so acute that this home-grown vegetable became a major staple of their diet. However, Germany and the Ottoman **Empire** imposed a successful blockade of their own on Russia in the Baltic and Black Seas.

Because of British naval power, the English Channel crossing between Britain and France was always open. Britain was able to import food and goods for its citizens and armies throughout the war. But Allied ships elsewhere faced a more serious threat from Germany's submarine fleet.

Two battleship squadrons of the German navy rest in Kiel Harbor on the coast of Germany. After the Battle of Jutland in May 1916, German warships never left their harbors in force for the rest of the war.

Mines and torpedoes

Warships were faced with weapons such as torpedoes and mines. Like armored battleships, mines and torpedoes were not strictly new to World War I, but both were used very effectively.

Torpedoes were originally invented in the mid-nineteenth century for ships, but became the principal weapon of submarines. They were missiles, launched through the water by ships or submarines to explode against the hull of an enemy ship. Powered by compressed air, they had a range of 5.5 miles (9 kilometers).

Mines were as terrifying a prospect at sea as they were on land. Consisting of a case of explosives, a mine could be laid anywhere, ready to explode at the slightest disturbance. Unexploded mines in the water, as on land, continue to be lethal hazards long after wars are over.

Submarines

Underwater war machines of one sort or another have been around since ancient Greek times. More recently, primitive submarines were used in the American Revolution. But it was a series of gradual developments in the nineteenth century that turned what was first a novelty into a formidable fighting machine.

Technological developments

Air-filled or water-filled ballast tanks that raised or lowered a submarine in the water were developed in the early nineteenth century. Torpedoes were invented in the 1860s. So was the **periscope,** a viewing device that enabled a submarine crew to see above water and make an attack from below. Powerful electric motors were introduced in the 1880s. (Previous sources of power, from oars to hand-turned propellers to steam engines, were not practical underwater.) By the early twentieth century, submarines were fitted with two engines: an electric one for underwater, and a cheaper, faster, diesel one for surface travel.

An effective weapon

With all the technology in place, nations such as Britain, France, and Germany began to add submarines to their navies. When war broke out, they proved immediately effective. One German submarine sank three British navy ships when the war was barely a month old. In 1915, a German torpedo sank a British passenger ship, the *Lusitania*. About 1,200 were killed, including 128 U.S. citizens. This attack led more Americans to favor entering the war.

German U-boats were dreaded by the Allies in World War I. They sank thousands of merchant and military ships. Yet for all their effectiveness, submarines were often coffins for their crews. Nearly half of all U-boat crews eventually went down with their submarines.

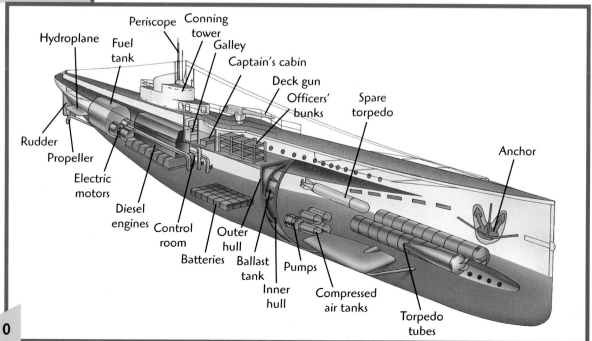

It was the submarine's use against merchant ships that was most effective, and it was Germany that devoted the most attention and resources to developing a submarine fleet for this purpose. A **blockade** against the powerful British fleet on the surface was not possible. But an underwater force nearly succeeded in starving Britain out of the war, as U-boats sank many merchant ships full of vital supplies.

The statistics prove the effectiveness of submarines, especially compared to other navy weapons. At the height of the sea war in 1917, German submarines sank 2,439 Allied ships, compared to only 234 sunk by German mines or surface ships. All together, German submarines sank nearly 5,000 ships during the war. These figures are even more remarkable in light of the fact that the German submarine fleet never numbered more than 140 vessels.

Two German sailors push a torpedo into the loading tube of a World War I U-boat, readying it for its next mission.

Surface ships fight back

When dealing with isolated merchant ships, a submarine crew would often surface and use its guns, since it was cheaper than using torpedoes. So, small merchant vessels called Q-ships were introduced. Armed with hidden weapons, they were ready to sink U-boats that surfaced to attack them. In 1916, underwater listening devices called hydrophones were developed. These could detect submarines by the sound of their motors. Once found, the submarines were attacked with depth charges, explosive-filled cylinders set to **detonate** at a certain depth. Anti-submarine **minefields** were also effective. In one anti-submarine minefield, 165,000 mines were laid across U-boat lanes in the North Sea and English Channel.

The most useful defense against submarines was the **convoy** system. Introduced in May 1917, at the height of German U-boat success, this tactic involved groups of cargo ships traveling together with a navy escort. This gave the U-boats just one chance to spot the ships, rather than the repeated opportunities offered if they traveled separately. And if they did attack a convoy, the U-boat crew could be sure of **retaliation.**

Airplanes

Following the Wright brothers' first powered flight in 1903, the pioneers of aviation were closely watched by military planners eager to make use of this new technology. Both the U.S. and French armies bought aircraft designs from the Wright brothers in 1908.

When war broke out in 1914, the armies and navies of the main combat nations had their own aerial units, each with around 150 to 300 aircraft. In the beginning, it was thought that these planes would be used for **reconnaissance** and **artillery** spotting.

Bombers

As the war progressed, however, other uses developed. Large aircraft with multiple engines—such as Russian Sikorskys, Italian Capronis, and German Gothas—were built to carry bombs. Such aircraft could attack cities hundreds of miles behind the **front lines,** although they were never used in large enough numbers to cause significant damage.

A British Sopwith Camel exchanges fire with German fighter planes above the **Western Front.** *These aircraft were called biplanes because they had two sets of wings, one above the other.*

Fighters

The most useful aircraft of all proved to be small, light, and highly **maneuverable** fighter planes such as the French Nieuport, German Fokker, and British Sopwith Camel. At the start of the war, enemy pilots fired at each other with pistols. Then heavy machine guns were fitted to cockpits, but they were clumsy and difficult to use. In 1915, the Fokker aircraft designers invented the synchronized machine gun. This had an interrupting mechanism, and could fire directly through the propeller blades at the front of the plane. It enabled a pilot to aim his weapon by lining up his aircraft behind his enemy.

Multiple uses

By 1917, all sides were using aircraft for reconnaissance and ground attacks, and as artillery spotters, bombers, and fighters. German planes attacked trenches in squadrons of up to 30 aircraft.

Although Germany generally had the most advanced aircraft, victory in the air war went to the nations that could produce the most aircraft. By 1918, Britain and France had won control of the skies. In the final battles of World War I, their aircraft played a major role in attacking German troops, both at the front and behind it.

In the course of the war, the airplane had changed from a wondrous novelty to an essential fighting machine. On the Western Front alone, there were 10,000 combat planes. But the cost in lives was terrible. Germany and Britain lost 50 percent of their pilots, and France over 70 percent. The majority of these men had been killed in accidents—either at the front or in training—proving the dangers of introducing new, barely tried technology into such a central combat role.

*The most famous of the flying aces was German Baron von Richthofen, nicknamed the "Red Baron," who shot down 80 enemy aircraft before he was killed in action in 1918. Richthofen commanded a unit called the "Flying Circus." He realized early on that the future of aerial combat lay in squadron **tactics** and teamwork.*

The first air force

In Britain, squabbles over resources for aircraft between the army and navy resulted in the formation of the Royal Air Force (RAF), the world's first independent air force, in 1918. Aerial units for other nations were generally part of the country's army or navy, and many still are even to this day.

The flying aces

The arrival of the synchronized machine gun heralded the era of the flying ace. Men such as Robert Little of Australia, William Bishop of Canada, Eddie Rickenbacker of the United States, and Mick Mannock of Britain became the war's most glamorous figures. In a war of inglorious mud and mass slaughter, they engaged in single combat like medieval knights, whirling and wheeling in a clear, blue sky. Their countries mourned them as national heroes if they were shot down.

Airships

To the **civilians** who lived in fear of their arrival, there was something deeply sinister about the German Zeppelin airships. These huge, lumbering beasts of the air—up to 650 feet (200 meters) long—would leave their bases at dusk, slip through the night sky to drop their bombs on cities, and then return before dawn. They were able to fly higher than the earliest fighter planes, but if an airplane pilot did locate one, he would be met by a hail of machine gun bullets from several of the airship's many gunners.

Bomb carriers

The Germans were very proud of their airships, invented by and named after Count Ferdinand von Zeppelin. They represented an impressive technological achievement. Lifted into the air by huge quantities of hydrogen gas carried inside a lightweight steel skeleton, they were propelled along by four gasoline engines at a speed of nearly 60 miles (100 kilometers) per hour. Most importantly, they could carry nearly two tons of bombs, far more than any other flying machine at the start of the war. Great things were expected of the airship. If anything was going to carry the war to the cities of enemy nations, and destroy their factories and homes, it was the Zeppelin.

Look out below

Zeppelin attacks by the German army were launched all over Europe, from Paris to Brest-Litovsk, and from Bucharest to Sevastopol. Navy Zeppelins concentrated on bombing Britain, in the hope of bringing the war to a speedy end by paralyzing British industry.

But the Zeppelin promised far more than it delivered. The first one to attack London, on May 31, 1915, dropped 89 **incendiary bombs** and

This Zeppelin carries the words "Gott Strafe England," meaning "God punish England." It was a slogan of the Germans in World War I. Because of this, the English word "strafe" has come to mean to attack or bombard, especially with machine gun fire from low-flying aircraft.

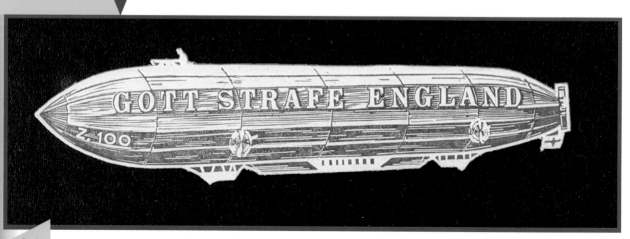

30 grenades on the capital's heavily populated East End. Yet only seven people were killed in the attack. Before the war, people had speculated that flying machines would bring large-scale destruction to enemy cities. But Zeppelin raids caused only minor damage.

Vulnerable targets

Their lack of effectiveness was only one problem. As aircraft technology advanced rapidly, fighter planes were soon able to fly as high as Zeppelins. Pilots discovered that incendiary (burning) bullets were perfect for setting alight the Zeppelin's highly inflammable hydrogen gas. When a Zeppelin caught fire it would light up the sky around it and turn its crew into blazing torches.

Zeppelins were also notoriously vulnerable to bad weather. In their campaign against Britain, 53 out of 77 of these huge machines were destroyed by storms, enemy aircraft and anti-aircraft fire before the German military called them off. Remaining Zeppelins were sent to the Eastern Front, where enemy aircraft were neither as numerous, nor as effective. There, they ferried supplies to German troops and continued to carry out bombing raids.

A Zeppelin is caught in searchlights in the course of a night attack over Britain.

Observation balloons

Hydrogen balloons were first employed in the early 19th century in the Napoleonic wars. They were immensely useful observation platforms. It was their use in the American Civil War that first gave Count Ferdinand von Zeppelin the idea of his huge mobile airships. In World War One, observation balloons would often be placed right behind the **front lines**. These balloons were prime targets for enemy fighters, so they were surrounded by batteries of anti-aircraft guns. Observation crews had such a dangerous job they were the only aerial combatants issued with parachutes during the war.

Communication

These women work in a British navy communications room. The woman on the left is using a radio, and the woman on the right is operating a telephone switchboard.

On the Balkan Front, two Turkish soldiers operate a field telephone from their shelter, a hole in the ground known as a foxhole. Although the telephone allowed for immediate contact, it also required long lengths of wire to be laid from one point to another.

The technology of electrical communication was still new when World War I began—the first radio transmissions were made in 1896, and field telephones were not used until the Russo-Japanese War of 1904–05. Radio and field telephones and **telegraphs** were utilized when possible in World War I, but more often than not, commanders had to resort to other methods. **Semaphore,** runners, highly visible rocket signals, and even carrier pigeons were all employed to carry messages to their **front line** troops.

Communication problems

The field telephone used an extended wire to connect front line command posts with headquarters behind the lines. The telephone was very useful because it allowed actual conversation, unlike the field telegraph. The field telegraph could transmit messages only in Morse code, a series of short and long sounds that correspond to the letters of the alphabet.

Transmitting Morse code messages under the stress of battle or bombardment was extremely difficult, however, and the wires for both telephone and telegraph were vulnerable to **shell** fire and other damage. Repairing them could be incredibly dangerous. Because all sides knew how valuable these communication links were, men sent to exposed spots to repair broken lines were prime targets for enemy **sniper** fire.

To compensate for this lack of effective communication, generals would often issue broad directives in advance to front line officers. But both generals and officers were unable to react with sufficient speed when circumstances changed in the course of battle.

Early use of radio

Radio, a form of communication without wires, was used increasingly in World War I. However, it had its disadvantages. Early radio sets were clumsy, fragile devices that were easily damaged. Radio signals could also be picked up by the other side. In 1914, the German army monitored Russian radio signals before the Battle of Tannenburg on the **Eastern Front,** and learned exactly what the Russians planned to do.

Secret codes were used, but they could be cracked, especially if code books fell into the hands of the enemy. Throughout the war, the British navy always knew what the German navy planned to do, because the British had a code book found on the body of a drowned German naval officer early in the war. Also, as radio use became more frequent, so did the jamming, or blocking, of radio signals. This was done by transmitting another noise that made the original signal impossible to hear.

This vehicle was used by the French as a mobile unit for carrier pigeons. The birds were trained to go to one particular location and then return. They carried messages tied to their legs.

Medicine

More than 12 million men were wounded in World War One. Injuries from bullets and **shells** were not new to medical officers, but the scale of the fighting often made treatment difficult.

Fighting infection and disease

On the Western Front, wounds rapidly became contaminated in the mud and squalor of the trenches. Antiseptics – chemicals used to keep wounds clean – were just not strong enough for the terrible infections and **gangrene** that resulted. Surgeons had to cut out the infection, and often cut off an infected limb altogether.

On the Eastern Front, disease was far more of a problem. There, a wounded man, his body struggling to keep alive already, was an easy target for any current **epidemic**. Millions of people died from diseases as there were no antibiotics to fight them.

Emergency care took place wherever it was needed, and field hospitals sprang up behind the front lines. The ruins of this bombed church in France provided shelter for the wounded and medical staff.

Gas casualties

Poison gas was a new challenge to doctors and nurses. Treatment was crude: cough medicines and the inhaling of medicinal vapours (steam) were used to ease damaged lungs. Doctors also used these to try and stop the build-up of fluids in the lungs which would slowly drown a man from the inside. Gas also caused a hideous form of infection in wounds known as gas gangrene. This was treated to an extent with injections to fight the poison, but again the surgeons often had no choice but to cut out infected flesh.

Helping the wounded

Dealing with wounds was a difficult task on the battlefront. But **technology** provided doctors with new tools for their patients. Portable X-ray machines, first used in 1898, allowed surgeons to locate bullets and shell fragments inside a wounded man. The discovery of the four main blood groups had been completed by 1900. This made blood

transfusions a much safer process, and medical stations commonly kept supplies of blood available.

Artillery fire, which killed more men than any other weapon of the war, also caused appalling injuries, particularly loss of limbs. The huge number of men who lost arms and legs encouraged development of more realistic and effective artificial limbs.

A wounded German soldier is X-rayed in a tent in 1916.

Plastic surgery

Facial injuries were particularly common in the trenches, as the head was the most exposed part of the body. The science of plastic surgery came of age during World War One. Surgeons, presented with a huge array of disfiguring facial wounds, made huge advances in restoring the features of injured soldiers. New techniques, such as skin and bone grafts, were developed. So were procedures for wiring together a shattered jaw. Missing bits of facial bone, vital to restore a man's appearance, were replaced by internal rubber splints. One pioneer of plastic surgery, Dr Harold Gillies of New Zealand, dealt with 2000 facial injuries during the Battle of the Somme alone.

Shell shock

A newly-recognized medical condition of World War One was shell shock, an all-purpose description for **psychological** breakdown. Shell shock was a particular feature of the Western Front because men were exposed to danger over such a prolonged period.

Soldiers suffering from shell shock may have no physical wounds but might shake uncontrollably, or be paralyzed, or have no control over their bowels and bladders. Front line medical staff and officers were suspicious of pretence and often quick to dismiss this condition. But gradually the idea that wounds of the mind were just as real as wounds of the body became accepted. Treatment varied from patience and sympathy to the use of electric shocks. Many victims were sent to psychiatric hospitals. Perhaps a quarter of a million men throughout Europe suffered from shell shock.

The Cost of the War

World War I came to an end in 1918. One by one, Germany and its cohorts surrendered, and Germany finally signed an **armistice** with the Allies on November 11.

One German **front line** doctor described World War I despairingly as "the suicide of nations." So many young men were killed that it became common to talk of "the lost generation." About 70 million men had been called to serve over the duration of the war. Of these, 37.5 million had been killed, wounded, or taken prisoner. The actual death toll was around nine million, so around one in eight of those who served had died. Nine million **civilians** died too, mostly from starvation and disease in the Eastern areas of the war.

From civilians to soldiers

What was so shocking about these losses, aside from their number, was that most of the dead had been civilians before the war: American farm hands, German factory workers, French peasants, British clerks, and Canadian school teachers. The war reached out its deadly fingers, plucked young men from their everyday lives, and destroyed them.

Thousands of miles from home, an Australian soldier carries his wounded comrade to a hospital in 1915, in what is now Turkey. Young men from all over the world became part of "the lost generation."

TROOPS KILLED IN WORLD WAR I	
AUSTRALIA	62,000
AUSTRIA-HUNGARY	922,000
BRITAIN	888,000
CANADA	65,000
FRANCE	1,300,000
GERMANY	1,800,000
ITALY	460,000
NEW ZEALAND	18,000
OTTOMAN EMPIRE	700,000
RUSSIA	1,700,000
UNITED STATES	116,400

The death toll on the **Western Front** was astronomical, but even more soldiers and civilians perished on the **Eastern Front.** The horrible scale of the slaughter was such that, on average, between five and six thousand people died for every day of the war's four terrible years.

Other costs of the war

The statistics of dead and wounded give only one aspect of the human cost of World War I. The men who died left widows and fatherless children. The maimed and **shell**-shocked—some reduced to begging in the street, others cared for by families or hidden in nursing homes and asylums—slowly faded away over the decades that followed. Many of the female half of the lost generation never married, whether from a simple lack of available men after the war, or from loyalty to those who died.

Memorials

Memorials to the fallen of World War I can be found in churchyards and village squares all over the world. Huge monuments and burial grounds mark major battlefields. For example, in northern France, where most of the fighting on the Western Front took place, tourists or pilgrims can visit cemeteries with mile upon mile of marble crosses. Many graves have names to record the final resting place for victims of what British Prime Minister Lloyd George called "the ghastly butchery of vain and insane **offensives.**" Among those buried are those whose shattered remains prevented any accurate identification. Their gravestones are marked "known unto God."

Rows of crosses at a military cemetery in France mark the graves of World War I soldiers. Most who died were under 30 years old, and many were not yet out of their teens.

The War to End All Wars

The end of pomp and glory
One British **front line** newspaper, the *Better Times*, spoke of the lack of excitement among exhausted and demoralized soldiers about the **armistice.** The paper's editor, Lieutenant Colonel F. J. Roberts, commented, "Most of us have been cured of any illusion we may have had about the pomp and glory of war, and know it for the vilest disaster that can befall mankind."

In World War I, pomp and glory disappeared for good. The technology used was either outdated or so new that it was still somewhat experimental, and therefore couldn't be used to its best advantage. During the course of the war, new **tactics** and weapons evolved. By 1918, the fearsome **offensive** power of airplanes and tanks was being used more effectively. In a future war, this new technology would make the deadly **stalemate** of the trenches less likely.

Good from bad
Not everything that came out of the war was bad. Nations had learned that to wage war on such a grand scale, they had to harness the entire industrial strength of their nation. The need for men at the front and for mass production of weaponry at home had led some nations to employ women in jobs previously held only by men. Women drove buses, delivered coal, operated farm machinery, and worked in **munitions**

*Radio capabilities developed during World War I were soon put to use in **civilian** life. By the late 1920s, when this photo was taken, radio sets were common in American and western European homes.*

factories. Although they did not fight, they worked near the front line as nurses, doctors, and ambulance drivers. As a result, men's ideas of what women were capable of were changed forever.

Technological advances, accelerated greatly by the urgent needs of war, had peacetime benefits too. The science that built bombers was applied to developing passenger aircraft instead. Newly introduced radio technology was used to create the world's first broadcasting organizations. Plastic surgery and blood **transfusions** became standard practices in **civilian** hospitals.

Deadly lessons

By the time World War I was over, it was being referred to as the "Great War" in recognition of the fact that human history had previously endured nothing like it. It was also called "the war to end all wars" in the hope that its horrors would never be repeated.

But this was not to be. One of the greatest tragedies of World War I was that it led directly to another war that would be even more terrible in its slaughter. As early as 1920, British journalist Charles A'Court Repington had coined the term "World War I." Like many other perceptive people at the time, he knew that the struggle between nations was not yet over. Barely twenty years after the Great War ended, military technology had been honed to even greater levels of murderous efficiency. The weapons of World War II would account for over four times as many casualties as in "the war to end all wars."

*A dead German gunner lies beside his machine gun at the end of the war in 1918. Light machine guns that were more useful as offensive weapons were developed during the course of the conflict. These guns became standard for **infantrymen** in World War II, enhancing their killing power in direct combat.*

Timeline

1896   First radio transmissions

1898   First portable X-ray machines used

1900   Discovery of four main blood groups completed

1903   First powered flight

1904   Field telephones first used (in Russo-Japanese War)

1906   Modern flamethrower invented

1914   June 28: Assassination of Archduke Franz Ferdinand

       July 28: Austria-Hungary declares war on Serbia

       August 1: Germany declares war on Serbia's ally Russia

       August 3: Germany declares war on France and invades Belgium

       August 4: Britain declares war on Germany

       August 14: French and German armies join battle in northern France

       August 26–31: Germans defeat Russians at Tannenburg

       September: French army stops German advance at Battle of Marne

       October/November: Trench systems established on **Western Front**

       November 5: Allies declare war on the Ottoman **Empire**

1915   Italy joins Allies

       Mark I tank developed in Britain

       Renault F17 tank developed in France

       Synchronized machine gun invented in Germany

       January 31: First use of poisonous gas on **Eastern Front** (at Bolimov)

       April 22: First use of poisonous gas on Western Front (at Ypres)

       May 7: German U-boat sinks British liner *Lusitania*

       May 31: First Zeppelin raid on London

       July 30: First use (by Germany) of flamethrower

1916   February–December: Battle of Verdun

       May 31: Battle of Jutland

       July–November: Battle of the Somme

       September 15: First use (by British) of tanks

1917   Mustard gas introduced

       April 6: United States declares war on Germany

       May: Allies adopt **convoy** system against German U-boat attacks

       June 7: Explosives **detonated** in tunnels under German trenches at
          Messines, France

       November 20: Tanks used successfully at Battle of Cambrai

       December 17: Russia signs truce with Germany and withdraws from war

1918   Royal Air Force established in Britain

       August 8: Allies launch final **offensive** against German army, leading
          to German defeat

       November 11: **Armistice** signed between Allies and Germany, ending
          World War I

Further Reading

Banks, Arthur. *A Military Atlas of the First World War.* Conshohocken, Penn.: Cooper, Leo Books, 1997.

Dolan, Edward. *America in World War I.* Brookfield, Conn.: Millbrook Press, 1996.

Gay, Kathlyn and Martin Gay. *World War I.* Brookfield, Conn.: Twenty-First Century Books, 1995.

Hull, Robert, ed. *A Prose Anthology of the First World War.* Brookfield, Conn.: Millbrook Press, 1993.

Kent, Zachary. *World War I: "The War to End Wars."* Berkeley Heights, NJ: Enslow Publishers, 1994.

Livesay, Anthony and John MacDonald. *Great Battles of World War I.* New York: Smithmark Publishers, 1997.

McGowen, Tom. *World War I.* Danbury, Conn.: Franklin Watts, 1993.

Rees, Rosemary. *The Western Front.* Chicago: Heinemann Library, 1998.

Ross, Stewart. *Causes & Consequences of WWI.* Orlando, Fla.: Raintree Steck-Vaughn, 1998.

Taylor, David. *Key Battles of World War I.* Chicago: Heinemann Library, 2001.

Glossary

ammunition bullets, shells, missiles, grenades and anything else fired during fighting

armistice agreement to stop fighting

armour plating thick metal sheets to protect a tank or ship, for example, against shells and bullets

artillery large guns that fire explosive shells

barrage barrier against an enemy action

barrel tube of a gun through which ammunition is fired

bayonet metal blade attached to a gun

blockade the use of warships to prevent other ships carrying goods or passengers to and from enemy ports

bunker underground shelter

canister metal container that can hold gas or ammunition

casualty wounded or killed person

caterpillar track revolving steel band, made up of joined sections, that is used instead of wheels for vehicles that travel on rough ground or in mud

cavalry soldiers who fight on horseback

civilian citizen of a country who is not in the armed forces

colony country or region ruled by another nation

convoy group of ships travelling together with an armed escort

counter-attack response to an attack

detonate make something explode

dug-out covered area dug into a trench for shelter

empire territory, usually covering more than one country or area, ruled by an emperor or other supreme ruler

epidemic disease spreading rapidly and affecting many people at once

fortify make stronger or add defences to. Fortified structures are known as fortifications.

front line the foremost section of an army's defended territory and the most exposed to the enemy

fuse device that sets off an explosion

gangrene condition where part of the body dies, and then rots, due to lack of blood circulation through the body tissues

home front situation or contributions of civilians in a nation at war

howitzer type of artillery that fires shells on a high trajectory

incendiary bomb bomb designed to set fire to buildings or other targets

infantry/infantrymen soldiers who fight on foot

infestation attack on the body by disease or insects such as fleas or lice

innovation something new or changed

latrine toilet in a camp or trench

magazine container for bullets attached to a firearm

manoeuvrable easy to move, turn or control in other ways

minefield area where explosive mines are laid

munitions ammunition, weapons and other equipment for fighting wars, used especially to mean shells

musket long-barrelled firearm used mainly in the 17th and 18th centuries

offensive used for attacking. Also means a large pre-planned attack.

outflank go round the side of an opposing army, so as to surround them or attack them from behind

parapet low wall built along the top of a trench to protect and hide troops

periscope instrument with which a person can observe from a concealed position, such as from a submerged submarine or over the top of a wall

pneumonia serious illness that inflames lungs and fills them with liquid

psychological to do with the mind

reconnaissance military observation to assess the strength and movement of an enemy

reinforcements extra support, such as new men or weapons brought into a battle

retaliation revenging an attack or injury with another

rifle long-barrelled firearm which has a rifled (spirally grooved) barrel. This spins the bullet being fired, to give it both longer range and greater accuracy.

round bullet and cartridge. The cartridge contains an explosive charge to propel the bullet from the gun, and is ejected once the bullet has been fired.

semaphore system of signalling using a flag in each hand, held in various positions to denote the letters of the alphabet

shell metal cases of various shapes containing explosives or other harmful materials

shrapnel form of explosive that violently scatters small pieces of metal; and the pieces that are scattered

sniper rifleman who fires from a hidden position, usually with a long range weapon fitted with a telescopic sight

stalemate situation where both sides in a conflict are unable to defeat each other

strategy overall plan for dealing with a conflict or in a battle

strongpoint defensive position on battlefront that has extra fortifications or weapons

tactic use of troops and moves made in battle

technology knowledge and ability that improves ways of doing practical things

telegraph device for sending messages along wires

trajectory path taken by an object as it flies through the air

transfusion injection of blood into a wounded person to replace blood lost in an injury

turbine engine engine driven by flow of liquid, gas or steam

turret small tower on a tank or ship that holds and protects guns and gunners.

velocity speed of an object's movement

war bonds certificates issued by a government during time of war to citizens who lend money to their nations for the war effort. The bonds promise repayment after the war with interest, which is extra money on top of the original amount of the loan.

Index